The science in...

...a glass of
WATER

The science of solids, liquids and gases and more...

Anna Claybourne

W
FRANKLIN WATTS
LONDON•SYDNEY

First published in 2008
by Franklin Watts

Copyright © Franklin Watts 2008

Franklin Watts
338 Euston Road
London NW1 3BH

Franklin Watts Australia
Level 17/207 Kent Street
Sydney, NSW 2000

Planning and production by
Discovery Books Limited
Editor: Rebecca Hunter
Designer: Keith Williams
Illustrator: Stefan Chabluk
Photo researcher: Rachel Tisdale

Every attempt has been made to
clear copyright. Should there be any
inadvertent omission please apply to
the publisher for rectification.

Dewey number: 530.4

ISBN: 978 0 7496 8236 1

Printed in China

Franklin Watts is a division of
Hachette Children's Books, an
Hachette Livre UK company.
www.hachettelivre.co.uk

Photo acknowledgements: istockphoto.com/Andi Berger,
front cover top; istockphoto.com/Alexander Hafemann,
front cover bottom left; istockphoto.com/konradlew, front
cover bottom right; Discovery Picture Library, p. 4 top;
istockphoto.com/Gene Chutka, p. 4 bottom;
istockphoto.com/Henk Badenhorst, p. 5;
istockphoto.com/Tatiana Grozetskaya, p. 6;
istockphoto.com/Graham Clarke, p. 7; CFW
Images/Michael Huggan, p. 9 top; NASA, p. 9 bottom;
Getty Images/Paul Nicklen/National Geographic, p. 10;
istockphoto.com/Anika Salsera, p. 12; istockphoto.com/
Celso Pupo Rodrigues, p. 13; istockphoto.com/Anna
Bryukhanova, p. 14; istockphoto.com/ddbell, p. 15; The
University of Georgia, p.16; istockphoto.com/Paul
Prescott, p. 18 top right; istockphoto.com/Paul
Vasarhelyi, p. 18 bottom right; istockphoto.com/
MaleWitch, p. 18 top left; istockphoto.com/Purdue9394,
p. 18 bottom left; Corbis/Bettmann, p. 19 left;
istockphoto.com/Sebastian Santa, p. 19 right;
istockphoto.com/Celso Diniz, p. 20; istockphoto.com/Bill
Grove, p.22; CFW Images/Edward Parker, p. 23;
istockphoto.com/Gerald Bernard, p. 24;
istockphoto.com/draschwartz, p. 27 top;
istockphoto.com/Sean Randall, p. 27 bottom;
istockphoto.com/Chanyut Sribuarawd, p. 28;
istockphoto.com/Klaas Lingbeek-van Kranen, p. 29

Contents

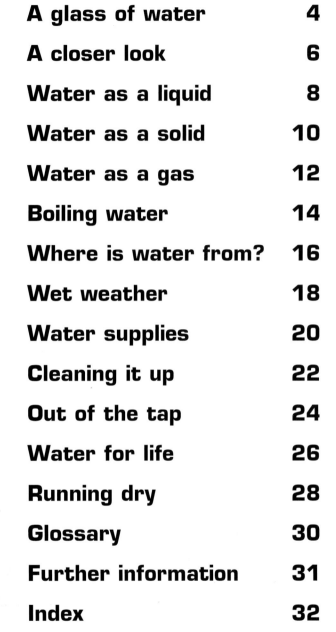

Words that appear in **bold**
are in the glossary on page 30.

A glass of water

When did you last have a clear, cool glass of water, or a drink with water in it? Maybe it's something you don't often think about. But water is one of the most important things on our planet. You couldn't live without it – and nor could anything else.

Amazing water

Water is a huge part of all our lives. Every day, everyone takes in several litres of it. (Even if you never drink a glass of water, it's there in your drinks and in your food.) It falls on our heads and houses as rain, snow, sleet or hail. It surrounds us in the vast seas and oceans. We sail on it, catch fish from it, and love to swim, splash and play in it. We rely on it to keep us alive, and so do all the Earth's living things.

▲ *You need to drink several glasses of water this size every day.*

▶ *Water is essential in our lives, but can be fun, too!*

▲ *A lot of water moving at once, like this large wave, can be very powerful and frightening.*

Dangerous water

Even though we need it, water isn't always good news. Too much water can cause serious problems. Floods ruin homes and crops, terrible **tsunamis** sweep away whole villages and towns, and rising seas swallow up the land. Water claims many lives by drowning, and dirty water can carry deadly diseases.

Water wonders

When you pour a glass of water, do you know where it comes from, or what it's made of? When you turn on the tap, water comes out – but how did it get there?

And why is there so much water on our planet in the first place? This book has the answers. It's all about what water is, why we need it, and the amazing things it can do. And it explores all the science and technology that goes into delivering water to your home, your tap and, finally, into the glass in your hand.

A closer look

A glass of water looks totally clear – but what is it actually made of? Like everything else, water is made of tiny bits called atoms and molecules. There are huge numbers of molecules in a glass of water.

Atoms and molecules

All the materials around us, such as water, wood, plastic and stone, are made of atoms. Atoms are tiny particles. They're so small that you can't see them. There are about 100 different types of atom.

Water contains two types of atom – **oxygen** atoms and **hydrogen** atoms.

▼ *As this stream flows, trillions and trillions of water molecules rush over its rocks every second.*

Atoms sometimes join together to make bigger parts called molecules. Water is made of water molecules. Each water molecule is made up of two hydrogen atoms and one oxygen atom.

How many?

Atoms and molecules are very small. A glass of water is made up of about 30 trillion trillion (30,000,000,000,000,000,000,000,000) atoms. As there are three atoms in each molecule, that's 10 trillion trillion water molecules per glass.

What else is in water?

Pure water contains just water molecules. It has no taste, smell or colour.

But most of the water in the world is not pure. The water in rivers and lakes is full of dirt, dead flies and leaves, and tiny living things such as **bacteria** and **algae**. Water in the sea is not pure either – it is very salty.

The water that comes out of a tap has been cleaned, but it still contains other substances, such as chemicals that are added to kill **germs**.

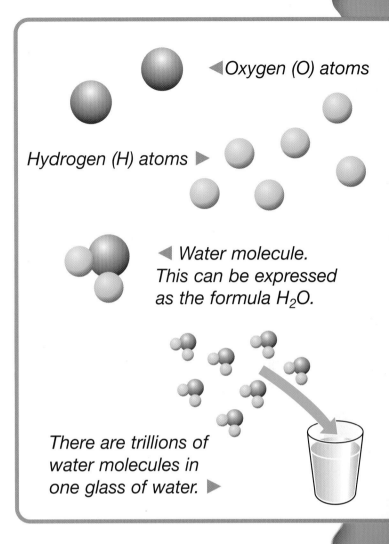

Oxygen (O) atoms ◀

Hydrogen (H) atoms ▶

◀ *Water molecule. This can be expressed as the formula H_2O.*

There are trillions of water molecules in one glass of water. ▶

Did you know?

There are more molecules in one glass of water than there are glasses of water in all the world's seas and oceans.

Water as a liquid

When you think of a glass of water, you think of a liquid. It can be poured into or out of a glass. You can splash it, spill it and drip it. But water can be solid too – when it gets very cold it freezes into ice. Water can also change into a gas and escape into the air.

Three forms of water

Water can take three forms – solid, liquid and gas. But what decides which form it is? The answer is its **temperature** – how hot or cold it is.

When water gets very cold, it freezes solid. The freezing point of water is 0°C.

When water is heated up, some of its molecules escape and float into the air as a gas, called **water vapour**. At a temperature of 100°C, water boils. It bubbles and steams, and eventually all of it will turn into water vapour.

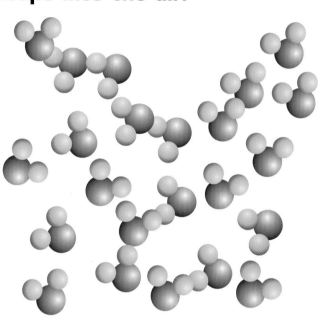

▲This diagram shows how the molecules in liquid water behave. They are close together, but they can move around easily.

What is a liquid?

In a liquid, molecules can move freely. They slip and slide against each other as they move around. That's why liquid water flows, forms puddles, and fills any container you pour it into.

Liquid planet

On most parts of the Earth, the temperature is usually somewhere between the freezing point and boiling point of water. So water usually exists as a liquid. That makes it easy for plants and animals to survive, as they can find plenty of liquid water.

▶When water is a liquid, it's easy for us and other living things to drink it.

The power to dissolve

Liquid water is very good at dissolving things. This means it breaks them down into molecules which combine with the water. Many drinks are mostly water, with other substances dissolved in them. These are called solutions.

Sometimes, substances can be suspended in water. That means tiny lumps of the substance are mixed into the water without dissolving. This forms a **suspension**. Muddy water is water with soil particles suspended in it.

Water on other planets

The other planets in our **solar system** have water on them, but they are mainly too hot or too cold for the water to be liquid. For example, Venus is very hot, and so water there is in the form of gas. Mars is much colder than Earth, and its water is frozen into ice. You can see some of the ice on the planet Mars at the bottom of this photo.

Water as a solid

On a hot summer day, you might add a few ice cubes to your glass of water to cool it down before you drink it. Ice is water that has frozen, or turned into a solid.

All about ice

When water is cooled to its freezing point, 0°C, it starts to become solid. As this happens, the water molecules stop flowing freely. They fix themselves together in a regular pattern (see diagram opposite). As they do this, they spread out a little, and the water **expands**. This means that ice is lighter than liquid water. That's why ice floats.

This is very unusual. Most substances shrink as they get colder. When they harden from a liquid into a solid, they get denser and heavier. Solid butter, for example, does not float on melted butter. It sinks.

Because frozen water floats, we get icebergs in the sea, and ice-covered lakes and ponds in winter.

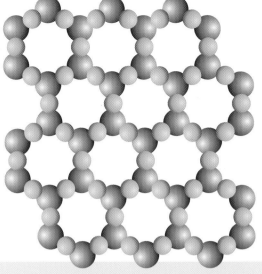

▲ The molecules in frozen water are locked together in a regular pattern, like this.

Why is ice slippery?

As you know, it's easy to slip and slide on ice. Why? Scientists have found that even very cold ice has a thin layer of water on its surface. A few molecules stay loose and flowing, like liquid water. This thin layer makes it hard for shoes and car tyres to grip the ice.

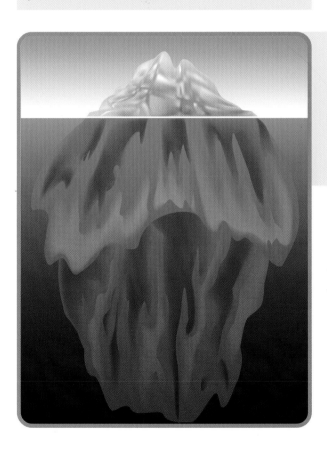

◀ When ice floats in water, about 90 per cent of it is under the surface, and 10 per cent above. This picture shows how much of an iceberg is underwater. Icebergs are a big danger to ships.

How water breaks rock

Did you know that water can split a rock into pieces? When it rains, liquid water seeps into tiny cracks in rocks. If the temperature drops below 0°C, the water freezes. As water expands when it freezes, it slowly pushes the cracks apart, making them bigger. Eventually, after freezing many times over, a piece of the rock breaks off.

This process is called ice weathering. Over many years, ice weathering can damage stone walls and statues, and even wear away mountains.

◀ An iceberg is a chunk of ice that has broken away from a glacier near the North or South Pole, and floated away into the sea.

Water as a gas

Water is all around you right now. It's not just in taps, pipes, rivers and lakes. It's also right in front of your face, in the air, in the form of an invisible gas called water vapour.

Evaporation

When water is heated to its boiling point, 100°C, it boils and turns to vapour. This is called **evaporation**.

However, water also evaporates at other temperatures. All the time, water molecules escape from the surface of liquid water and become water vapour in the air. The warmer the water is, the more easily it evaporates.

Air is normally about 1 per cent water vapour – but it can hold more or less water. When there is a lot of water in the air, it is said to be very humid.

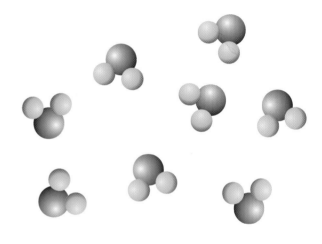

▲ In water vapour, as in other gases, the molecules are spread far apart and zoom around at high speed.

◄ Wet clothes dry faster if you hang them up in the sunshine, or on a warm radiator. The heat helps the water to evaporate.

Seeing your breath

Have you ever been outside on a very cold day and seen your own breath, looking like steam? What you see is the water in your breath. Normally the water vapour in your breath is invisible. But in cold air, the water vapour starts to **condense**, forming tiny water droplets that are visible as a cloud.

Condensation

When water vapour gets cold, it starts to condense, or turn back into a liquid. You can see condensation happening if you take a cold drinks can out of the fridge on a warm day. Water vapour in the air condenses onto the cold can, covering it with liquid water droplets.

Sweating it out

It takes **energy** to make water molecules break free from liquid water and become water vapour. The molecules take this energy in the form of heat from their surroundings.

Our bodies use this fact to help us cool down when we get too hot. Our skin releases liquid sweat, which sits on the surface of the warm skin and starts to evaporate. As the sweat evaporates it takes heat from the skin, and the body cools down.

Did you know?

In one hot day, a man's feet can release enough sweat to fill a whole glass.

▼ *Water vapour from the air has condensed and collected on these cold cans.*

Boiling water

In prehistoric times, people found that food is easier to eat, and it tastes better, when it is cooked. We often use boiling water to cook things. We use it for a lot of other useful things, too.

Heating water up

Look around your home or school, and you'll see plenty of uses for boiling water. Stoves and kettles boil water for making hot drinks and cooking food. You may also have a boiler which heats up water to fill radiators around the house, and to give you hot water for baths and showers.

Why does heat cook?

If you try to eat a raw potato, it is rock hard and not very nice. But cook it in boiling water for 20 minutes, and it's soft and delicious. What happens? When food heats up, the chemicals in it change. Often, heat makes the molecules in food break apart and form new chemicals. This can change the form and flavour of the food.

▲ We boil water to cook food in our kitchens every day.

The heat of boiling water also kills germs. If you think drinking water might be unclean, you can boil it to make it safer to drink.

Natural boiling water

Most water in the wild is pretty cold – but water does boil in nature. Around volcanoes, hot, molten rock in the ground heats up underground water, creating boiling hot **springs**, mud pools and **geysers**. At the bottom of the oceans, super-hot boiling water escapes from the seabed at **hydrothermal vents**.

Useful energy

Did you know that most of our electricity is made by boiling water, too? Power stations use machines called **generators**. They convert the turning motion of a wheel into an electricity supply. But how do they make the wheel turn? The easiest way is to boil water to make steam. The steam pushes at a **turbine**, making it whirl around.

▲ *A geyser is a natural boiling water fountain. Hot rock heats up water in an underground pool until it boils and shoots out of the ground in a giant jet.*

▼ *In a power station, fuel is burned to boil water to make steam. The steam makes a turbine turn, and a generator converts the turning motion into electricity.*

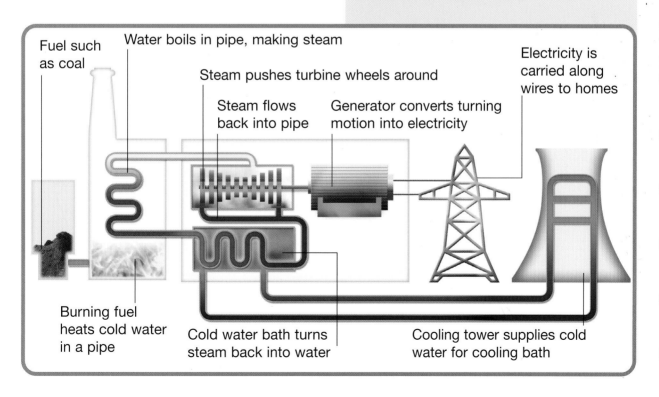

Fuel such as coal

Water boils in pipe, making steam

Steam pushes turbine wheels around

Steam flows back into pipe

Generator converts turning motion into electricity

Electricity is carried along wires to homes

Burning fuel heats cold water in a pipe

Cold water bath turns steam back into water

Cooling tower supplies cold water for cooling bath

Where is water from?

Of all the water on Earth, 97 per cent of it is in the seas and oceans.

Where is the water in your glass from? Water comes from the tap, and the water in the tap comes from rain. But where did it come from before that? Where did water come from in the first place? The answer is outer space.

How much water?

Altogether, there are about 1.4 billion cubic kilometres of water on Earth.

- 97 per cent of that water is in the seas and oceans.
- 2 per cent is frozen into ice around the North and South Pole and on high mountains.
- 1 per cent is liquid **fresh water**, found in rivers, lakes, underground and as water vapour in the air.
- One glass holds about 250 ml of water. So there are about 5,600,000,000,000,000,000,000 glasses of water on Earth!

Water and the world

Scientists think the Earth began about 4 billion years ago. It formed when dust, rocks and hot gases in space clumped together to make a planet. One of these gases was water vapour. As the new planet cooled down, the water vapour turned into liquid water. It fell as rain and collected on the Earth's surface.

More water came from comets – balls of rock and ice that fly through space. Some comets hit the Earth, and the ice in them melted, adding to the planet's water. Over two-thirds of the Earth's surface is covered in water.

Seas and oceans

Most of the world's water – 97 per cent – is in the sea. The Earth is covered in a layer of rock, or crust. All the water on Earth flows downwards, pulled by gravity. Over time water has filled the places where the Earth's crust is lowest, forming the seas and oceans.

▼ *This diagram shows a simple version of the water cycle. Of course, water also evaporates from rivers and lakes, but mostly from the sea.*

The water cycle

However, water doesn't just stay in the sea. It is constantly moving around from one place to another in a pattern, called the water cycle. The picture below shows how the water cycle works.

Ancient water

The water cycle has been happening for billions of years. The water in your glass could have satisfied the thirst of an ancient Greek or a dinosaur!

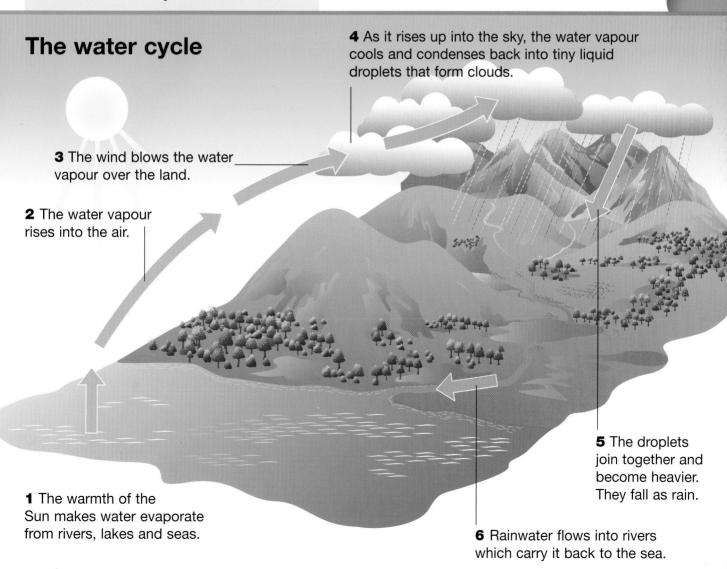

The water cycle

3 The wind blows the water vapour over the land.

2 The water vapour rises into the air.

4 As it rises up into the sky, the water vapour cools and condenses back into tiny liquid droplets that form clouds.

5 The droplets join together and become heavier. They fall as rain.

1 The warmth of the Sun makes water evaporate from rivers, lakes and seas.

6 Rainwater flows into rivers which carry it back to the sea.

Wet weather

Water usually falls from the sky as rain. But it can also fall as snow, sleet or even hail. Dew, frost and fog are all made of water, too. Water plays a huge part in most kinds of weather. Any form of water falling from the sky is called precipitation.

Cloud shapes

Clouds are made of water vapour that has started to condense into tiny water droplets. The droplets are not heavy enough to fall to the ground, but they are big enough to catch the light. That's why clouds look like fluffy puffs of steam or smoke.

Clouds form different shapes, depending on the weather and how high up they are.

Stratus clouds are wide, flat layers that block out the sun.

Thin, wispy cirrus clouds form high in the sky.

Nimbus clouds are low, dark clouds that will soon bring rain.

Cumulus clouds float lower, and look like cotton wool.

When rain freezes

If the air is below freezing, rainwater can freeze before it reaches the ground.

Snowflakes form when tiny droplets of water freeze into delicate ice crystals. As they float around in the

▲ *Each snowflake has a six-sided symmetrical shape but no two snowflakes are ever exactly identical.*

▲ *In a serious ice storm, a thick layer of ice can build up on surfaces and objects, like this tree.*

air, more droplets freeze onto them, building up a six-sided pattern. Because snowflakes are mostly air, snow is soft and fluffy.

Hailstones are hard, heavy balls of ice. They form inside thunderclouds, when water freezes around specks of dust. Layers of water build up, making the hailstones bigger and bigger, until they fall to the ground.

Dew, frost and fog

Sometimes when you wake up in the morning, the ground is wet although it hasn't rained. This is dew. It forms when water vapour in the air condenses onto the cold ground. If it's very cold, dew can freeze, making frost. And if water vapour condenses into little droplets in the air, it creates fog or mist.

Ice storms

An ice storm happens when liquid rain falls onto freezing cold ground. As the rain hits the ground, it freezes solid. Everything gets covered with a layer of heavy, slippery ice. The ice can make people slip and cars skid. It can also weigh down trees, roofs and power lines until they break.

Rainbows

Even rainbows are made of water! When you see a rainbow, you are looking at sunlight shining through raindrops. The curved shape of a raindrop makes the white sunlight split into a range of colours.

Water supplies

Have you thought about what happens to a glass of water before it flows out of your tap? It doesn't get there by magic! It has to be collected, stored, cleaned and then piped all the way to your house.

Collecting water

We use big, artificial lakes called reservoirs to collect and store water before it is used. That way, there is always water ready to use, even when the weather is dry.

Most reservoirs are made by building a dam across a river. A dam is a strong wall that holds the water back, creating a big lake.

Dams – good or bad?

Dams can be both helpful and harmful. As well as creating reservoirs, they can be used to make electricity. At a **hydroelectric power** plant, water is let through a dam at high speed. The water turns a turbine, and a generator converts this turning power into an electricity supply. Hydroelectric power is considered to be good

▼ *This is the Hoover Dam, on the Colorado River in the western USA. It runs a hydroelectric power plant, as well as supplying water to cities such as Las Vegas and Los Angeles.*

Water from the sea

In some dry countries, there is so little rain that people cannot get enough water from rivers or from underground. Instead, they take water from the sea. It has to be **desalinated** before it can be drunk.

Water from the ground

As well as flowing into rivers, rain soaks deep into underground rocks. Water stored underground in this way is called **groundwater**. We can collect it by digging wells down to where the water is, and pumping it up to the surface.

for the environment, as it creates little **pollution**.

However, building a dam can also be bad for the environment. Huge areas of land need to be flooded with water. This ruins natural **habitats** for wildlife. Some dams destroy towns and villages as well.

Down the pipe

Most reservoirs are higher than the towns and cities they provide water for. The water can easily flow downhill through pipes to get to where it is needed.

▼ *This cross-section diagram shows how a hydroelectric dam works. Water flows through the dam and turns a turbine to make electricity.*

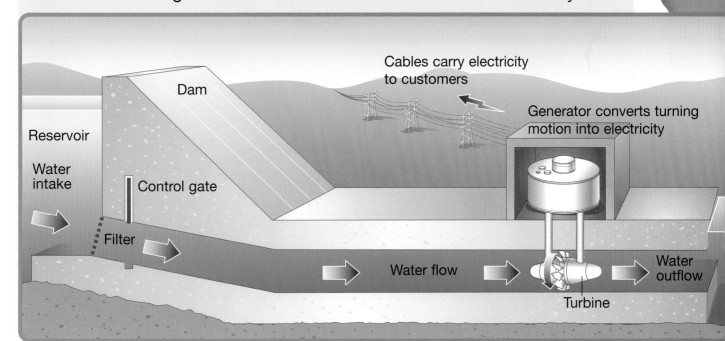

Cleaning it up

Before it arrives at your tap, dirty water from a reservoir must be cleaned at a water treatment plant. There, the water goes through several stages before it is safe to drink.

Screening and settling

First of all, the dirty water has to be screened. This means it is passed through a big sieve or strainer that catches twigs, bugs, leaves and litter.

Filtering out the bits

Next, special chemicals are added that make dirt stick to them. The dirt in the water clumps together and the lumps slowly settle and sink to the bottom. The water is still not completely clean, so it is now filtered. The water sinks slowly through layers of sand and carbon (a black substance found in coal and on burnt toast). The carbon soaks up germs and smells, while the sand filters out the tiniest particles of dirt.

The clean water passes on to the next stage.

▼ *A water treatment plant seen from the air.*

Germ killer

The water is nearly ready, but before we can drink it, a chemical called chlorine is added. This is the same chemical that is added to the water in swimming pools, although there is much less chlorine in drinking water than in swimming-pool water. Chlorine kills germs in the water.

Sometimes, other chemicals are put in too. For example, some drinking water contains added fluoride, a chemical that helps to keep our teeth healthy.

Into the mains

From the water treatment plant, the treated water flows into the mains water pipes. These are big underground pipes that carry water around cities and towns so that it can be delivered to every building.

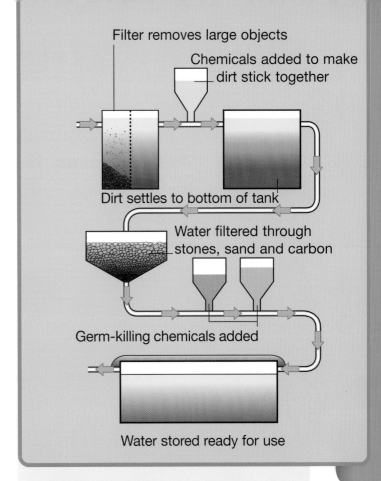

Filter removes large objects

Chemicals added to make dirt stick together

Dirt settles to bottom of tank

Water filtered through stones, sand and carbon

Germ-killing chemicals added

Water stored ready for use

▲ *This diagram shows the different stages water goes through as it is being cleaned.*

Untreated water

Long ago, everyone collected their water straight from a river or well. In some parts of the world, people still have to do this, as their countries are too poor to build water treatment plants and pipes to supply everyone. This water does not get treated and often causes illness and disease.

Out of the tap

So you turn on the tap, and pour out a clean, sparkling, delicious glass of water. But how did the water get from the mains to your tap – and how does water flow to the rest of your home?

Plumbing

Plumbing is the system of pipes that carries water into and around your home. A water pipe branches off from the water mains to take water into your building. It is connected to pipes leading to all the taps in your home, such as in the kitchen and the bathroom.

There are also pipes leading to your shower, your central heating boiler, your washing machine and toilet.

How a tap works

The water in the mains is under pressure, so it is constantly pushing its way up into the plumbing pipes. So why doesn't water flow out of the taps non-stop? When a tap is off, it is sealed shut by a part called a washer inside it. When you turn the tap on, this part moves, opening up a gap that lets the water through.

◀ *We're used to turning on the tap to get water any time we like – but now you know how much work goes into getting it there!*

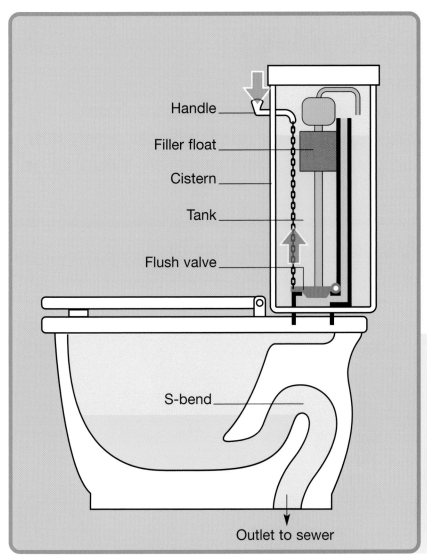

Handle
Filler float
Cistern
Tank
Flush valve
S-bend
Outlet to sewer

◀ *This cross-section diagram shows one common modern flushing toilet design. When the handle is pressed, the flush valve lifts up to let water empty into the toilet bowl.*

Toilets

A toilet has a bowl of water linked to a curved pipe, called an S-bend. The S-bend traps some water in the bowl, so that it can't drain away. A toilet also has a tank called a cistern that fills up with water.

When you flush the toilet, the cistern empties all its water into the bowl. It sweeps away the waste through the S-bend, and fills the bowl with clean water again.

Down the plughole

When you pull the plug out of your bath, or flush the toilet, the dirty water is carried away down a waste pipe. This dirty water is called sewage, and pipes that carry sewage away are called sewers.

Sewage is piped to waste treatment plants, where it is filtered and cleaned. The water can then be emptied into seas and rivers, or piped back into the water supply to be used again.

Water for life

Now you know where a glass of water comes from – but do you know what happens to it after you drink it? Water keeps your body working, and does all kinds of useful jobs inside you.

Water in your body

When you swallow water, it goes down your throat and into your stomach. From there, it goes into your **intestines**. These are tubes that soak up water and food through their walls and carry them into your blood.

Blood is mostly made of water. It is pumped around your body by your heart and carries oxygen and useful chemicals to all your body parts.

Your **cells** need water too. They have to be bathed in water to work properly. The tiny parts inside cells can only move about and do their jobs if they can float around in a watery solution.

◀ *Did you know that you are mostly water? The human body is around 70 per cent water. However, it does not slosh around like water in a bucket – it is spread out around your body and stored in your cells, blood and other body fluids.*

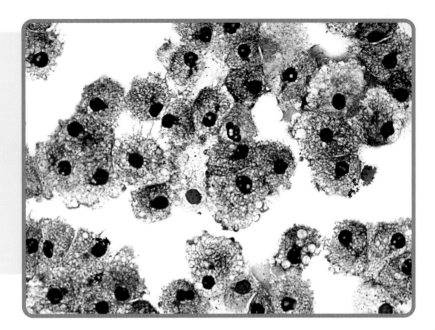

▶ *These are human white blood cells seen under a microscope. Each cell is filled with a jelly-like substance which is mostly made of water. There is water around and between the cells too.*

Losing water

You lose water from your body all the time. It comes out as sweat, saliva (spit), tears and as water vapour in your breath. Your body also makes urine to carry waste chemicals out of your body. Because of this, you need to drink plenty of water every day.

Animals and plants

It is not just humans that need water. All living things depend on water to stay alive. Animals, like humans, drink water, while plants use their roots to get water from the soil.

Desert survival

Some desert animals, such as camels, can go without drinking water for weeks! Camels are very good at storing spare water in their bodies. They also save water by sweating very little.

Running dry

New people are born every day, and they all need water. But in many parts of the world, clean, fresh water is starting to run out. We are using it up more quickly than we can replace it.

Using too much

There is a vast amount of water on Earth – far more than we could ever use. But most of it is salty seawater, and some is locked up in ice. Only about 1 per cent is fresh liquid water.

We have seen that the total amount of water in the world doesn't change, it just gets recycled round and round in the water cycle. So why are we now in danger of running out? Our problem is that the way we live uses up more and more clean water.

Agriculture and industry use huge amounts of water and are extremely wasteful. It takes 1,000 tonnes of water to produce 1 tonne of grain. If we look at all the fresh water in the world, 69 per cent is used in agriculture and 23 per cent in industry. This leaves only 8 per cent to supply all the people in all the towns and cities in the world.

In some countries it won't be long before the clean water supply runs out.

What's the answer?

Many experts think that as water shortages get worse, we will have to turn to seawater. Desalination is already used in some countries (see page 21). It will probably become much more common during the 21st century.

However, there are problems with desalination. It is expensive and uses up lots of energy. It also makes the sea saltier (as the extra salt gets left behind). Wildlife in the oceans may not be able to adapt to saltier seas.

In the future, governments may have to ration water, by making laws to limit how much each person can use.

Did you know?

More than one billion people in the world today – nearly one seventh of the world's population – do not have access to a clean water supply.

What you can do

You can help to save water supplies by using water carefully.
- Don't leave the tap running while you clean your teeth or wash your face.
- Have quick showers, not deep baths.
- Collect rainwater or used bathwater to water your plants with. Don't use a garden hose.
- Don't pave over your garden to make a driveway – keep it as grass or soil. This allows rain to soak deep into the ground, to become groundwater.

◀ *It takes between 1 and 4 cubic metres of water to produce 1 kilo of rice! Since over 600 million tonnes of rice is produced worldwide every year, that's a huge amount of water being used!*

▲ *The Middle-Eastern country of Kuwait is famous for its unusual and beautiful water towers. They store seawater that has had its salt removed to make it safe for drinking.*

Glossary

algae tiny plant-like living things

atoms the tiny particles that all matter is made up of

bacteria tiny living things that can sometimes cause diseases

cells very small units that living things are made of

condense to turn from a gas into a liquid

desalinate remove the salt from seawater

energy something that makes things work. Electricity, sound and light are all forms of energy

evaporation turning from a liquid into a gas

expand to get bigger

fresh water water that is drinkable and not salty like the sea

generator a machine that converts turning motion into a flow of electricity

germs tiny living things that can cause diseases

geyser a jet of boiling water from under the ground

groundwater water held in rocks underground

habitat the place where a living thing makes its home

hydroelectric power (HEP) electricity made by using flowing water to turn turbines

hydrogen one of the basic elements, or substances, found on Earth, and one of the two ingredients of water

hydrothermal vent a hole in the seabed where hot, boiling water escapes from inside the Earth

intestines tubes inside your body that soak up water and food chemicals

molecule a single particle of a substance, often made of several atoms joined together

oxygen one of the basic elements, or substances, found on Earth, and one of the two ingredients of water

pollution harmful chemicals, waste gases or dirt released into the environment

solar system our Sun and the planets and other objects that circle around it

spring a place where groundwater flows out of the Earth's surface

suspension a suspension is made of lumps of a solid mixed into a liquid

temperature how hot or cold something is

tsunami a powerful, fast-moving wave that can swamp the coast, causing disaster

turbine a wheel that can be turned by steam, flowing water, wind or other forces in order to produce electricity

water vapour water in the form of a gas

Further information

Websites

Water Kids
http://www.water-ed.org/kids.asp

Children's information site from the Water Education Foundation.

Water Science for Schools
http://ga.water.usgs.gov/edu/

The US Geological Survey's water facts site.

Water for All
http://www.oxfam.org.uk/education/
resources/water_for_all/water/
gettingstarted.htm

Oxfam's site to help school groups learn about water use.

Note to parents and teachers: Every effort has been made by the Publishers to ensure that these websites are suitable for children, that they are of the highest educational value, and that they contain no inappropriate or offensive material. However, because of the nature of the Internet, it is impossible to guarantee that the contents of these sites will not be altered. We strongly advise that Internet access is supervised by a responsible adult.

Index